WRITTEN ON THE WIND

THE

POEMS & PROSE

OF

JUNE HELEN FLEMING

June Helen Fleming

FERNHOLM PUBLISHING

WRITTEN ON THE WIND

THE POEMS & PROSE OF JUNE HELEN FLEMING

FERNHOLM PUBLISHING
Post Office Box 89
Winfield MO, 63389-0089 U.S.A.
Orders @fernholmpublilshing.com

All rights reserved. No part of this book may be reproduced in any form or by any means, electronic or mechanical, including photocopying, recording or by any information storage and retrieval system without the permission from the author, except for the inclusion of brief quotations in a review.

Copyright © 2011 by June Helen Fleming

First edition: ISBN: 10: 1-883165-73-3
ISBN: 13: 978-1-883165-73-4
Printed in the United States of America

Cover and book design by June Helen Fleming

Library of Congress Catalog card Number: 2010938386

Publisher's Cataloging-in-Publication
(Provided by Quality Books, Inc.)

Fleming, June Helen.
    Written on the wind : the poems & prose of June Helen Fleming. -- 1st ed.
    p. cm.
    Includes bibliographical references.
    LCCN 2010938386
    ISBN-13: 978-1-883165-73-4
    ISBN-10: 1-883165-73-3

    I. Title.

PS3606.L464W75 2011   811'.6
                                   QBI10-600222

WRITTEN ON THE WIND IS DEDICATED TO:

My husband Bob, our son Kim, and our daughter Rhonda

My sister and her husband
May and Lawrence Othmer

My Friends

Delia Garcia,
Francisco Garriga
Garry Vickar
Joanne and Kevin Gordon

To those who inspired me

Celine Dion
Josh Groban
Kris Kristofferson
The Moody Blues
Neil Diamond
Bob Dylan

TABLE OF CONTENTS

THE POEMS

1. A WHISPER IN THE WIND
2. BECAUSE I LOVE YOU
3. UNDER THE CHERRY TREE
4. THOUGHTS OF YOU
5. YOUR BROKEN HEART
6. GOD'S RAINDROPS
7. MISSING YOU
8. TEARS
9. A TOUCH OF HEAVEN
10. I WISH I WERE IN LOVE
11. MY LITTLE WHIP-POOR-WILL
12. TO DR VICKAR THE HEALING HAND
13. MOTHER TERESA
14. DARK CLOUDS
15. TO JAMES - A SOLDIER I KNOW
16. IT IS TIME TO GO NOW
18. JOY PAIN AND SORROW

19   DON'T WAIT

20   MY LTTLE HEART IN ETERNITY

POEMS FOR CHILDREN

25   MY TEDDY BEAR

27   ALONE

28   TO MY LITTLE ONE

29   PRECIOUS CHILD

30   TOKENS OF YESTERDAYS

31   AUTUMN ROSE

32   THE PLAYGROUND

MOTHER

37   MY DEAR MOTHER - ETERNAL YOUTH

38   A LAST GOOD-BYE TO MOTHER

PROSE

41   THE FORGOTTEN ORCHARD

42 PASSING BY

43 MY TRUE ANGEL STORY

47 THE PATH OF FRIENDSHIIP

DEDICATED TO MY DEAR MOM AND DAD

50 TO MY DEAR MOM AND DAD

DEDICATED TO MY SISTER

59 A SPECIAL DEDICATON TO MY SISTER

65 TO MY CHILDREN

ABOUT THE AUTHOR

I have been writing poetry and prose for many years. When I was a little child in public school, my teachers sent us to the school library to choose a book to read. I always came back to my classroom with a book of poetry. I dreamed that someday I would be blessed to be a poet. I never thought it would take so many years to write my first book of poetry.

It took many years for me to accomplish my dreams. I had to go through many experiences, good, bad, and very sad, to get to that place where my poems came easy to me. It seemed that every experience brought out a poem. I have always been a very sensitive person, in tune with nature. Love of my family brought out several of my poems.

Now that my poems are finally written down for all to read, I like to think of them as written on the wind, because they are forever with me, like the wind.

I was a child of the depression. I was born in a little house on View Street in Haileybury, Ontario, Canada, now called Temiskaming Shores. My parents lost that home in the Great Depression. My family moved to Cobalt, Ontario. I try to go back to Cobalt every year. I am thankful for the place that shaped my life for the future. This place is sacred to me. It is like the temple of my soul. All my childhood dreams are there. The home I grew up in on Lang Street is still there. I feel the presence of my parents who have been gone for many years. My sister May still lives in Cobalt, and wonders how I could ever leave and go so far away.

I hope everyone who reads my poetry will enjoy it, and find a poem that has special meaning to them.

WRITTEN ON THE WIND

THE POEMS

A WHISPER IN THE WIND

When clover covers the fields
And dandelions bloom in the spring
Will I just be a whisper in the wind

When the evening breeze caresses the trees
And moonlight fills the sky
Will I just be a moonbeam in your eye

When raindrops kiss your cheeks
And pitter-patter on your heart
Will I just be a raindrop in your eye

When ocean waves caress your feet
Where we used to stroll
Will I just be a seashell in your hand

So hold me close and never let me go
I feel safe in your arms
Don't ever let me go or I fear
I will just be a teardrop in your heart

BECAUSE I LOVE YOU

You may send me away
With tears in my eyes
But I will return
Because I love you

You may cast me away
When you are too busy
To be with me
But I am always there when you need me
Because I still love you

You find time for others
And leave none for me
But I sill love you

The darkest night
Could not hide my love for you
You became part of a burning flame
Because I love you

Love has no boundaries it has no place to hide
It is everlasting and eternal in the hearts of those who
Love with their heart and soul
Love hurts and love lives eternally
May you have the blessing of love in your heart

UNDER THE CHERRY TREE

When the cherry blossoms bloom in the spring
I will stand under its branches
And remember your tender kiss

When the blossoms fall like snowflakes
Around me
I will remember your tender smile

When the leaves fall to the ground
Around me
I will be there
Remembering you tenderly
In my heart

And when the cherry blossoms bloom again
And fall
My heart will be in deep sadness remembering
Your eternal love

THOUGHTS OF YOU

A poem a song a sunset
Makes you
Only a heart beat away

A sigh and you are there in
My heart
Touching my soul
With your sweet memories

The pain and sorrow
I feel in my heart
Is sometimes too much
To bear

I will spread my tears
Throughout the years
Thinking of you

YOUR BROKEN HEART

You are one star too far
I'd climb the Milky Way
To mend your broken heart

Please forgive me dear
I didn't mean to go so far away
I'd climb the Milky Way
To mend your broken heart

I see your crying eyes
In all my dreams
I'd climb the Milky Way
To mend your broken heart
We are just one star too far

GOD'S RAINDROPS

When memories
Are painful
Tears fill our eyes

God waters our garden
With tears
From our eyes

MISSING YOU

I try not to miss you
My sad heart cries for you
Longing for the days gone by
I hear your gentle voice
I look and you are not there

Your soft steps haunt me
I know you are somewhere
I try not to care
Missing you

TEARS

I feel your tears of sadness
As if they were mine

I'll drown in your sorrow

A TOUCH OF HEAVEN

I think I saw a touch of Heaven
One day
When my heart was heavy bent
God's window opened up
And sent a ray of light

A rainbow to my heart

I WISH I WERE IN LOVE

I wish I were in love
I'd float upon a cloud
I'd sing a merry tune
I wish I were in love

I'd paint a sky of blue
And put the stars up for you
I wish I were in love

I'd ask the birds to sing
I'd welcome in the spring
I wish I were in love

When autumn comes again
And leaves fall to the ground
I wish I were in love

When winter snow covers the ground
And frosts the window panes
I wish I were in love

When spring returns again
And the birds begin to sing
I wish I were in Love

MY LITTLE WHIP-POOR-WILL

He soars over the meadows
Early in the morning to find a place to rest
At night he rests on branches high
In the shadow of the moon

I love that little whip-poor-will
He charms my heart at night

TO DR. VICKAR THE HEALING HAND

Seagulls and Eagles fly high
Kim Lee Seagull was a wounded Seagull
Who wanted to fly like an Eagle
His days were numbered

Frightened and lonely
He tried to find a way
To mend his broken wing

One day a powerful
Healing hand touched his Life
And Kim Lee the Seagull
Took off for the sky

MOTHER TERESA

Precious Mother
Of love and Care
Who smiled on us from afar

You touched our hearts
With God's love
And lifted us from despair

DARK CLOUDS

Dark clouds circled over his head
He almost wished that he was dead

Then you touched his soul
And gave it life
And let the sun shine through the clouds

TO JAMES - A SOLDIER I KNOW

A soldier I know
Came back from the war
He served his country well

A soldier I know
Left his home for two years
To fight for his country
He served his country well

A soldier I know
came back from the war
And
Could not go back

Can you understand
I can
A soldier I know could not go back
To the war
He lost his soul
And now he has to find it again
Can you help him
I wish I could
Can you

IT IS TIME TO GO NOW

When you are happy, I am happy.
When you are sad, I am sad.
It is time to go now
I see it in your eyes,
I hear it in my heart,
That you are leaving soon.
My life will never be the same
When you are gone.
I will hear your foot steps.
You will be in every thought
And every prayer.

I shall miss you,
You are sunshine when all is gray,
You are my rainbow, full of love
You are a special gift from God.

You are a soft breeze
That fills my heart.
You are earth you are sky.
You are eternally with me.

God crafted you and molded you
Into a perfect soul,
And gave you to me because
He knew you were special
And I would look after you for Him.

Now it is time for God
To send you on your mission.
I don't know what path He has chosen for you,
But I know that it is something special that
You must do for Him. It is time for you to go now.

You must seek what I could not find.
Love with all your heart and follow
God's love and wishes all the days of your life.
The path will be daunting at times my son,
But you will travel along the golden path
And the sun will shine on your face.
I will always be in your heart and at your side;
You are a child of God and you are mine.

JOY PAIN AND SORROW

The gifts of life are joy and pain and sorrow

Sometimes we reach a place in life
When fear and pain take over
And as hard as we try to reach for our dreams
Our life shatters around us

God help us through our pain and sorrow

DON'T WAIT

Don't wait
You may be too late
Say it while you can
Don't wait

Moments pass
And they are gone forever
Don't wait
You may be too late

You pass this way but one time
Don't wait
Say it now
Don't wait

When souls depart
It is too late
Say it now
Don't wait

Eternity is a long time
Say it now
Don't wait
You may be too late

MY LITTLE HEART IN ETERNITY

Two hearts beating under the daylight sun
When midnight came one little heart was gone
Never to be on earth again

I pray in God's care
The little heart will stay
And someday I shall see
The little heart that left me

Life has its moments of sadness
Life has its moments of joy
You brought me joy for such a short while
When your little heart was beating within me

The day your little heart left me I was sad
But someday I will meet you in Heaven
And our hearts will be as one

I pray until that day comes
God will keep you in his care
And in eternity we will share our love again
Oh how I miss your little heart beating within me

This is a sad moment in my life
You could have filled it with joy
But you are gone now
Never to be with me on earth
I will always think of your little heart beating within me
I pray God will keep you in his care
Until I see you someday in eternity

God forgive me for my sorrow
God forgive me for what could not be
Someday I will see you in eternity
I shall always miss your little heart beating within me

WRITTEN ON THE WIND

POEMS FOR THE CHILDREN

Amanda our granddaughter

MY TEDDY BEAR

When no one else is there for me
You are always there

I hold you close at night
I know you'll stay with me until morning light
Because you are my teddy bear

Sometimes I take you shopping
Because I don't want to leave you alone
When you are with me
I don't mind leaving home

I dress you up in funny clothes
And show you off to folks
You never seem to mind
Because you are my teddy bear

Rhonda and Kim our children

ALONE

I found you sitting alone
What were you thinking dear
Your deep silence hurt me
You had nothing to say
I felt so very much alone

I wanted you to smile
And say I love you dear
All is forgotten now
Come sit by me I care

TO MY LITTLE ONE

I held you in my arms
When you cried
You were safe there
It was for such a little while
Oh my little one how I miss you

Yesterday I thought about you
How you ran to my side to feel safe
I see your face in all my memories
Your beauty lingers in my mind

The joy you gave is beyond all time and space
You are the essence of my soul
You are part of me
You are eternal

When I kissed you good night and covered you up
You looked contented and you knew I was there
I think of you now and wish I could cover you up
And kiss you good night one more time and
Know that your little heart belongs to me
Just one more time

PRECIOUS CHILD

Oh precious child
Your eyes tell all
Your deepest secrets
Lie deep within your soul
God grant you peace
For what you've done
You broke my heart my little one

I hold your grief within my heart
Our souls are one today
Your hurt lies deep within my soul
God grant us peace this day

TOKENS OF YESERDAYS

Little tokens of yesterdays
Linger in my mind
A wooden star hand painted
With the moon and the stars

A loving token from a little granddaughter
Left here for me

Precious tokens of yesterdays surround me

Little notes tucked here and there
With grandma I love you
Are so special in my mind
A loving feeling in my heart
Lingers for yesterdays

Precious tokens of yesterdays surround me

AUTUMN ROSE

The last little Rose of Autumn
Lingered in the morning sun
Dew drops from Heaven
Nourished her
Hoping she would get strong

As the Autumn days went by
Her petals began to fall
One by one they touched the earth
Sadly falling to the ground

Winter came and she rested
Snowflakes covering the ground
And the little Autumn Rose lie silent in the ground

We all mourned and missed her
Sadness filled our hearts
When Springtime came
My Little Autumn Rose bloomed again
In Heaven

THE PLAYGROUND

The playground is empty now
I can still hear the laughter
And see the smiling faces
Of the happy children
At play

I see them come down the slide
And quickly run up and come down again

I ponder now for the moments of days gone by

And oh how I miss the days that will
Never come again

Candice
Candice and Amanda

Amanda, Casandra and Candice our granddaughters

WRITTEN ON THE WIND

MY MOTHER

My dear Mother Helen

MY DEAR MOTHER - ETERNAL YOUTH

I followed you down the road
You skipped merrily on your way
Youth was by your side

The day was sunny and bright
No clouds were in the sky
Youth was by your side

The autumn leaves fell down
You felt them brush your cheeks
Youth was by your side

Winter came and frosted your cheeks
You had a rosy glow
Snowflakes kissed your cheeks
You felt youth by your side

Now the seasons have come and gone
And many will not come again
But in your heart youth is by your side

A LAST GOOD-BYE TO MOTHER

Her sad eyes beckoned mine
As if to capture the lifetime
We shared
There was very little time left now
To say good-bye
Her tear filled eyes made me sad
I knew our precious moments together were fading fast

What time do I have left to say good-bye
I love you
My dear mother
Don't worry about me
I will be okay
I will miss you everyday

I will kiss yours tears away dear mother
And they will be tears of joy
In heaven

I love you

WRITTEN ON THE WIND

THE PROSE

THE FORGOTTEN ORCHARD

I once took an interesting walk into a forgotten orchard. As I strolled along I could see the beauty of every little living thing. As my imagination grew, I could hear a voice say,

"I am an orchard centuries old. I have many a tale I could tell, if I were only alive like people are. I am only living in soul. The curtains of night have fallen often upon me, and after the darkness has fallen, I await the dawn. The dawn comes with the awakening of the sun to a lovely new day, bringing life into my orchard. I used to have people visit me and take care of my trees and flowers, but now I am forgotten by all. My wild flowers grow up to meet the sun, to escape the tall dangling vines, and paths of weeds. My tall trees hang in twisted vines. It is a place of solemn stillness. Then I heard the voices of my trees whispering, and the songbirds singing. We are forgotten by all but our Creator."

I then looked up at the sky above me and at the trees. They were nodding and rustling their leaves. I knew then as I gazed around me at every little, living thing, that the voice I heard was truly the voice of the forgotten orchard

PASSING BY

It was quite a calm day, as I watched farm after farm pass by from my car window. Tall elms reached for the sky that sheltered farmhouses from the cold winter winds. It was early spring. Many fields were newly ploughed ready to plant. Nearby a windmill stands still, waiting for a friendly breeze. A red barn caught my eye, bringing back memories of times I spent at my grandfather's farm. Memories tugged at my heart, I longed for days gone by. The sun was trying to come out to meet the day. Smoke rose in the distance from a farmhouse over another hill, as clouds hid part of it. Silos stood proud holding the last of winter's grain, and patches of wild flowers took over the fields. It was time to plant again.

Small clusters of trees and bushes, looking like little forests, passed by as my eye caught broken fences, here and there that needed mending. My eye caught a horse waging his tail in a peaceful pasture as cows grazed. I was just passing by.

MY TRUE ANGEL STORY

My mom and I started out early in the morning to make it to her doctor appointment, forty-five miles away. We liked to stop at McDonalds close to the doctor's office, to have a coke, and a cup of coffee before her appointment.

Upon entering McDonalds, I went up to the counter and ordered our drinks while mom found us a sunny, cheery place to enjoy them. We always liked to have a little time to talk about what we are going to write next. Mom and I both like to write poetry. I am always telling her she must write because the world needs her poems. My mom's poetry touches peoples' hearts.

After I arrived at the booth mom picked out, I sat down with our drinks only to find my mother looking very upset. Suddenly, I could see what was bothering her. She was listening and paying close attention to a man sitting alone taking to a tall policeman. This poor man was being questioned about his well being.

I asked my mother what was going on? We wondered if this man was in trouble with the law. I felt that he looked too innocent for it to be anything serious. Mom and I listened closely to the conversation trying to figure out what was wrong with this stranger.

We now could see that his clothing was wet and he was shivering. He had such a chill that he could hardly talk. It was a very cold morning to be sitting with a wet coat and pants. We noticed that his boots were wet and covered with mud, We could clearly see that some kind of accident or something strange had happened to him.

The day manager, a middle-aged lady brought him a cup of hot coffee while they tried to find out what had happened to this poor soul. He appeared to be able to answer the questions that the policeman was asking him. Overhearing the questions, we were certain he was trying to determine if he was mentally sound. We could hear most of the conversation. He not only was wet but he had some kind of injury. Finally, the policeman asked him if he could take him to his home. It seemed like he was telling them he had fallen in the river, and got wet, and hurt his back, while trying to take a short cut to McDonalds. He kept telling the policeman that he would be okay. The manager tried to convince him to let the policeman take him home. Finally, the policeman said he would not be able to take him home at this time, and that he would send another police car for him, because he had another call. Mom and I felt that he was afraid to go with the policeman.

My mom kept looking at her watch and saying, "I have to go soon to my appointment or I will be late." She looked me in the eye and told me not to take him anywhere until she returns. Mom knew me well because we both think alike when someone is in need of help. I assured her that I would be here waiting for her when she came back from her appointment. Just as she was about to leave, another policeman turned up.

My mom felt all would be okay now, and she left saying good-bye, telling me again not to go anywhere without her. I assured her that I would be here waiting for her.

Upon returning my mother found me talking to the stranger.

Mom was not too surprised as she said to me. "He has a sweater just like the one that I bought you with the American flag on it." My mom suddenly looked at me and could see that I was not wearing my lovely dark blue sweater with the flag on it. It was no surprise to my mother. She would have done the same. I told my mother that I had finally convinced the stranger to take off his wet coat by asking him if I could have it. He gave it to me out of kindness, and I got him to put my warm sweater on. I could see that he finally had stopped shivering. Mom asked me why the second policeman didn't take him home? The policeman could not take him home because he was a canine unit, and could not take someone in the car with the police dog. My mom and I both thought this was ridiculous. It was clear to us that this man needed to get to his home, and get some dry clothing on.

After talking to this stranger for a few more minutes, he had gained our trust and decided that he would let us take him home. I told my mom to sit and talk to him while I went for our van. I returned and I asked the stranger if he was ready to go home now. I told him that I have my van ready to take him home. I helped this poor old man up from the cold wet booth and took him by his arm. He could hardly walk. I had to lift one of his feet at a time into the van. We asked him if he would let us take him to the emergency. He said, no he would be fine. He said, he lived on Flamingo Drive. After turning several corners, and listening closely to his directions, we arrived at what he said was his home. I helped him out of the van one foot at a time, and took his trembling arm. He stopped and started to take off my sweater. I said, "no you keep it to remember the strangers that were sent to help you." I Helped him to his door and he reached into his pocket and the key he held in his hand opened the door.

We were thankful that we were able to get him home. We returned to McDonalds to tell the kind manager that we got him home okay. She thanked us and we left feeling happy that he was safe and warm.

Mom reminded me of the TV Show "Touched by an Angel." This is what this day is all about. Mom said, "don't you feel like God put us here to help this stranger today." I then felt like we were really God's Angels that day. I guess we all are at times. God puts us where He needs us.

THE PATH OF FRIENDSHIP

We have worn a long path of friendship across the country field, to each other's door. Corn fields have come and gone as we made our way to each other's home. Clover and dandelions line the path, each spring always there reminding us that another season has come. New life comes each Spring with the fresh sent of country air, perfumed with the smell of sweet clover. Butterflies and bees land on the wild flowers while the morning birds sing to welcome the day, as I arrive to the aroma of fresh coffee made by my dear friend

Summer arrives, and our path is getting narrower, as the tall grass and weeds grow up on both sides of the narrow path, that our footsteps have made over the years. I know that fresh coffee is always waiting for me, with a friendly welcome from my dearest friend.

When autumn breezes come catching the last clinging leaves falling from the surrounding trees, I kick my boots through the leaves, and feel them crunching under my feet. I feel like a child again as I scurry along. The air is getting brisker now there is almost a chill of winter in the morning air. My friend's coffee will be welcome when I arrive.

I'm Scarf clad with tuque pulled down over my ears. I trudge along the path, trying to follow yesterdays footprints in the winter snow. With my boots full of snow, I arrive with rosy cheeks and nose. Now my friend and I sit by the fire she made in her cook stove. I take off my boots and wet socks, and warm my feet on the oven door. Then we drink our fresh morning coffee reminiscing about our childhood days of frozen feet and toes.

Now many years have passed, and when I pass by our old farm houses the path has grown over, and my friend no longer lives at the end of the path of friendship. A feeling of loneliness overcomes me knowing that those days will never come again.

WRITTEN ON THE WIND

DEDICATED TO

MY DEAR MOM AND DAD

HELEN DOLAN FERNHOLM
1909 - 2000

ADOLF FERNHOLM
1900 - 1964

TO MY DEAR MOM AND DAD

I placed a few of my favorite photographs of my parents in my book, because I wanted them to be remembered by those who loved them deeply as my sister May and I.

Now that our parents have been gone for a long while, my sister and I often talk about how wonderful our parents were. We reminisce about all they did for us, and appreciate how they raised us. We ask each other if we thanked them enough for all the years they worked hard to make it possible for us to have a better future than they did.

When the great depression came we lost our home in Haileybury, and so did my grandparents who lived across the street from us.

The stone quarry where my dad worked, no longer needed him because, of hard times, and, he was unable to find another job. He was blind in one eye since he was four years old.

I remember the day that we were told to leave our home. I was about five years old. All our furniture was put out on the front lawn of our house. My sister May is a year and a half older than me. We found blankets amidst the pile of stuff in the yard and, we took blankets and placed them over the chairs, in the yard and made a tent. I don't know if we thought we would be sleeping in our tent that night.

Our friends from across the street came over with a picture of their family, and gave it to me, so that I would not forget them. I still have it. It is part of a childhood memory that I hold close to my heart. Teresa was my little friend in the picture. Many years later I tried to find her, and I found out that she became a nun.

My grandfather found a place to rent in Cobalt, a town five miles south of Haileybury. We moved in with my grandparents, for a short while, until my dad got a job working underground in one of Cobalt's silver mines. My parents found a house across Cobalt Lake for us to live in. It meant that my sister and I had a very long walk to school. In the winter we walked across the lake, and it was bitter cold. Sometimes the temperature reached forty to sixty degrees below zero.

My dad would snowshoe us a path across the lake when the snow got too deep for us. He got up early before he had to go to work, and made us a path. When we got across the lake, we had to walk the railway tracks for a long distance. When spring came we had a longer walk, because we had to walk around the lake and then walk the tracks. There were no school buses in those days or school lunches. We did without until we got back home.

Finally my mother found a home for sale on Lang Street. It was an old mining cabin from the early silver rush days. The log walls were so thick you could sit on the windowsills in the kitchen. They bought it for fifty dollars, because it was such a depressing looking place. It was directly across from the Catholic school, in what they called French Town. The walls were lined with v-joint lumber and painted battleship gray. The upstairs had been added on, and there were two bedrooms up there. My sister May and I shared the front bedroom that looked out on Lang Street. Across the street was the Catholic school where the sisters lived. When I looked out my bedroom window I could see the nuns walking around the school early in the morning saying their prayers on their prayer beads. It was a peaceful sight. I felt sorry for them in the heat of the summer with their long black garments, and their heads covered up. They wore a white piece across their forehead that looked very uncomfortable

Little did I know that at the time one of the nuns would become very fond of me? My mother purchased a piano for fifty dollars from the second hand store, and I was to take piano lessons, and so I did. Her name was Sister Barnard. Sister Barnard would watch for me coming home from the public school, and I would follow her around the school watering her flowers. I was about six years old then. When Sister Barnard left I had another nun for a teacher, but I could not understand her. She didn't speak English very well, so my mother found me another piano teacher near my school.

I wanted to play the violin like my dad, but when my dad placed the violin up to my chin and told me to reach the violin string on the far side of the strings. I could not reach them so daddy said you will take the piano lessons.

The music lessons were an added expense for my mom and dad, but nothing was too good for us. We would take lessons even if it was their last cent.

I had to take piano exams from the Toronto Conservatory of Music each year. I practiced many long hours and at last my old piano started to fall apart. I would take it apart and fix it myself. We were taught there was no such word as can't.

When my sister and I were in high school, her music teacher had a concert orchestra, and he asked me to play in it. They had a piano player, so I ended up playing the drums, and I played in the percussion section too. My sister played the violin in the strings section. I grew to love playing in the orchestra. I miss it to this day, because my sister May and I enjoyed playing in the orchestra together.

My mother made all of our clothing. We were dressed alike. People thought we were twins. There is a picture of my sister May and I among the daisies near the end of my book. You will see us in the same dresses

We were allowed to have dogs, and horses. I have always had a dog. I have a white German Shepherd now. Animals teach children compassion and caring.

May and I grew up in a peaceful home. Our parents never spanked us or hit us. My mother talked a lot when she felt she had to, but only in kindness. The family home we grew up in is still on Lang Street. I go by to see it when I go home. The roof is caving in, I don't know if anyone is living in it now. My sister and I lived there until we left home, and my parents lived there for many years after. It was our home.

How could children raised with such caring parents not be thankful that they were our parents. What a wonderful life they made for us. When my mother ended up in the hospital for three months. I went home and spent everyday at the hospital with her. I told her every day how much I loved her, and let her know what a wonderful mother she was to us. I was happy that my sister, and I could be there for her, because she was always there for us. We were not able to be with my dad on his last days, because he went to work two days after Christmas, and took a heart attack at work and died. I was happy that I was with him Christmas day. I tell everyone that my dad died with his boots on like a soldier. He was my hero, and still is. They are forever with me in my memories.

WRITTEN ON THE WIND

DEDICATED TO MY SISTER

MAY

WITH WHOM I SHARE

MANY WONDERFUL MEMORIES

I LOVE YOU

My sister May and me

A SPECIAL DEDICATION TO MY SISTER MAY

I don't know where to begin to tell you how much you mean to me, because our lives have been so entwined. We have been together since we were little children. The years we spent together are precious, and meaningful to me. How fast time has gone by. It is good we made so many wonderful memories to share.

We walked deep snow trodden paths, through the long days of winter, on our way to school. When spring came, and the Chinook winds from the prairie blew across the land, it tanned our faces, and gave us hope, that the long winter days would soon be far behind us.

We were proud of our school, we always wore our long bright blue and gold ribbons, pinned to our clothing when we left for school. It was important to display our ribbons at all times, and especially at the rugby games held at our school. There was a lot of cheering, and ribbons flying in the wind. Those were the good days to remember. You could tell which school was cheering for their team, because they displayed their ribbons proudly. We felt very patriotic to wear our ribbons.

I remember the good times we had in late spring and summer. Mom and dad planted a garden every spring, so we would have food for next winter. Daddy had an old car that he cut in half and made into a truck. It was our transportation to our ten acres of land that was given to my father by his dad. There was a little shack on the ten acres where mom and dad kept their garden tools. You and I had to go along with our parents every weekend and work in the garden, although we were not much help. We mostly stayed out of their way. Sometimes we ran across a farmers pasture, to visit our cousins, who lived near by. It was a bit scary because we had to watch out for a big bull that was in the pasture. He chased us one time, and our little dog Trixy saved us from the bull. We were able to get over the fence to safety, because she was a brave little dog, and barked so hard at the bull. She was fearless in order to save us from the charging bull.

We climbed up on top of the old shed, and laid there on our backs gazing at the sky, to share our dreams. When Sundays came, a few of our close friends would turn up, and pile into dad's old truck, to go along with us to the garden. We all thought it was the best time we ever had, including mom and dad. They had to start bringing extra lunches along to feed the hungry bunch.

Our grandmother lived not too for from us. I remember the days we would go over to grandmas, and ask her if she would make us a blueberry pie, if we picked some berries. She found us a few baskets to put the berries in, and off we would go. It did not take us very long to get to where the blueberries were on the hills behind her house. We had to go down the back stairs at grandmas, and there was a very large rock hill to climb, and that is where we found the berries. We would climb carefully, because the rock hill was very steep. After we had enough berries we would return with the berries, and grandma would make a couple pies. My gosh they were very good.

I often think of a special teacher we had in public school. She was a medical doctor, and decided to teach school. She didn't have any children, and she liked you and me, because we liked to draw. She would let us come over to her apartment after school, and allow us to use her art materials.

We did some dangerous things. It was good that mom and dad did not know about them all. Remember when we took long walks to the different mining properties, and walked on the air pipelines that carried compressed air to the silver mines. Some of the big pipelines were up several feet high going over dangerous drop offs. It seemed like a lot of fun. We were too little to know the danger.

In winter we would put on our skis, and ski across the country mining roads, up and down the hills. It was so much fun. We would get so tired we could hardly make it back home. During the long winters we went to many hockey games, and spent a lot of time at the rink skating when they were not practicing for a hockey game. I loved skating more than you did, because every winter we had an outdoor rink at the back of our school, and I would stay and skate with my friends.

When we were both finally in high school together, I was happy to be there with you. I hated it when I had to walk to the public school without you. I felt very lonely and I missed you.

Now that we were big sisters together, in the grown up world of high school, you had already made new friends, while I was in public school.

I still had my friends from public school in my class, and soon adjusted to the change. We could still walk home from school again together. A few times our dog Laddie got out, and followed us to school. The winters were so cold our gym teacher would let us bring Laddie in. One time we went out a different door of the school, and when we got home Laddie was not there. We had to walk all the way back to school to find him laying by the door waiting for us. It was a long walk to make over, but we missed our Laddie. He was so faithful. There is a picture of me and Laddie in my book for our memories. We will never forget him.

I enjoyed the years that we played in the orchestra together. Those were very special times we spent together. I miss those years, and I bet you do too.

When you graduated from high school, and went to work as a teller, at the bank in town, I was proud of you, but I did not like to walk to school again without you. I guess that is what made me decide to go to New Liskeard to business school. It was a change and I liked it. I had to get up early, and take the bus to New Liskeard. I made a few new friends while I was at the school.

Although we took different paths, we still remain two lucky sisters, that still love and care about each other. Whenever I hear the song Silver Bells, at Christmas, I shed a few lonely tears, remembering when you bought your little record player with one of your paychecks, and you only had enough money to buy one record, and it was Silver Bells. Silver Bells tugs at my heart strings and lets me known how much I miss you.

Now that our parents have been gone for a long time, I am thankful that we have each other. Although circumstances brought me to another country to live, far away from you, we are only one moonbeam away. I can look out my window, and see the same moon in the sky that you see, and I long to see it with you again. I am thankful to have you for my loving sister. I love you my dear sister May, always and forever.

LADDIE & ME

TO MY CHILDREN

I will be with you until we meet again
When the wind blows I will touch your cheeks

My spirit will abide by the streams
When the water ripples over the rocks
I will touch your soul
When you gaze to the mountain tops
look for my spirit

When the autumn leaves rustle in the wind
I will hear you call my name
I will be lonely for you

HOW TO ORDER BOOKS
FROM FERNHOLM PUBLISHING

Check my website: fernholmpublishing.com
You will find instructions for ordering books on my website.

Email orders: FernholmP@aol.com

Postal orders: Fernholm Publishing
PO Box 89
Winfield, Missouri, 63389-0089

Sales tax: Please add 6.475% for books shipped to Missouri addresses.

Shipping by air

USA: $ 4.00 for first book add $ 2.00 for each addition book,

Send check or money order made payable to Fernholm Publishing to the address above.

NEW POETRY BOOKS

TITLE: WRITTEN ON THE WIND
SUB TITLE: THE POEMS & PROSE OF JUNE HELEN FLEMING
AUTHOR: June Helen Fleming
ISBN: 10: 1-883165-73-3
ISBN: 13: 978-1-883165-73-4   LCCN: 2010938386
PRICE: USA $ 14.99

TITLE: BLUEBERRY MOON
SUB TITLE: THE POEMS & APHORISMS OF KIM LEE SEAGULL
AUTHOR: Kim Lee Seagull
ISBN; 10: 1-883165-72-5
ISBN: 13: 978-1-883165-72-7   LCCN: 2010938385
PRICE: USA $ 19.99